True Nature Stories

by
V. Cameron

© 2006 V. Cameron. All Rights Reserved.

No part of this book may be reproduced, stored in a retrieval system, or transmitted by any means without the written permission of the author.

First published by AuthorHouse 01/20/06

ISBN: 1-4208-9157-X (sc)

Printed in the United States of America
Bloomington, Indiana

This book is printed on acid-free paper.

authorHOUSE

1663 Liberty Drive
Bloomington, Indiana 47403
(800) 839-8640
www.authorhouse.com

Dedication

Dedicated to my husband Jim, whose belief in my abilities enabled me to complete this project. He was an endless source of support and encouragement. Without his hard work, these wildlife adventures could not have taken place.

Special thanks to Carol Acker, who prompted me to tell my stories in writing.

Acknowledgements

Editor, Betty Dobson of InkSpotter Publishing.
Technical Advisor, David Gough of Gough's Stock Photography.

Introduction

The first time I heard from—or of—Vicki Cameron was through an unexpected message on my voice mail. She needed a book edited and found me through an Internet search. Several e-mails and telephone conversations later, we struck a deal to work together on preparing *True Nature Stories* for publication.

I quickly discovered a kindred spirit in Vicki. We are both outspoken, independent, and share a good sense of humor.

I also learned, through her written word, that her love of nature is deep and abiding. What her pictures cannot express—short though that list might be—her stories bring into sharp focus.

True Nature Stories is a loving collection of fireside tales, running the gamut from humor and peace to adventure and suspense. Even a fearful encounter with a black bear resonates with a healthy respect for nature.

If you've read this far, don't stop now. Even if you only look at the pictures, you'll still come away from this book richer for the experience.

A Blue Jay Named Fred

His claws held onto my forefinger, and we looked at each other eye to eye for what seemed the longest time. Then he snapped his head down and slowly ate the food from the palm of my hand. Between each bite, he always made eye contact with me. I could feel only the pressure of his little body through his claws, which didn't feel at all uncomfortable. This surprised me. His face was fascinating and distinctive. He had tiny, feathered eyebrows and quite a long beak, giving this wild blue jay the look of a stern eagle.

This memorable encounter was the result of a seven-year relationship. As he returned to me that day many times over the period of an hour, I thought back on how this relationship had begun. Winter hiking was relatively new to me, during one of those winters when there was some snow but not enough to completely cover the wooded hiking trails (Nova Scotia is renowned for its unpredictable winters.) The day was clear, sunny, and cold, and I was really looking forward to getting out for a hike after a hard week of working.

My husband Jim, with his usual flair, had a bag of potato chips to bring along and "of course" there would be sharing. We parked our truck at the beach, and I took my third appendage—the camera. We hadn't gone more than a few steps into the trail when I heard the raucous call of a blue jay. Initially I paid no attention. The bag of chips had been opened by then; as we walked along we passed them back and forth. The calling persisted turn after turn, which piqued my interest. I realized he wasn't going to leave and, to be honest, I perceived the loud calls as breaking the wonderful solitude of the forest. Amidst hearty laughter, I mockingly held up a potato chip in my hand and yelled out to him, "If you're so hungry, come and take this."

As I stood there in total amusement, the jay quickly swooped down and took the chip from my upraised hand. Both Jim and I were totally floored. He had been a surveyor and a seasoned woodsman but had never seen anything like that from a wild blue jay in his career. On the off chance this might have only been a fluke, I tried the action again—and again the blue jay took the chip from my hand. We walked along repeating this activity until he flew away. I was to learn later we had left his territory. We completed our hike and returned on the same path. Would he still be there? He was, complete with a repeat performance. We were tickled. This particular hike was grounds for many lighthearted conversations and fond recollections.

We went back the following weekend, driving two and a half hours each way from the city. (Being hooked on the great outdoors sometimes requires a lot of diligence.) We parked in the same place and set out on the same trail. By then, the snowless winter had ended—and the temperature had dropped considerably. The snow squeaked as I walked on it, and the inside of my nostrils would freeze ever so slightly as I would inhale. I stood there in the cold, crisp snow and called to the blue jay. Just when I thought I had been entirely too optimistic, I could hear the flutter of his wings as he flew towards us from the depth of the woods, tree by tree. Same call, same response—what a treat! This time I'm thinking "camera," however he wasn't going to stay around for a photo shoot. I had to find a way to get him used to me.

By the third weekend, we were hooked. I soon picked up on this bird's presence when our red truck would pull in. I decided to see if I could feed him at the parking lot—no easy task. That February was bitterly cold. Having my bare hand exposed for any length of time was incredibly painful, but the blue jay was faithful, so I persevered. The time had come to figure out how to get this on record. The plan was to have me position the camera up by the truck with settings ready and Jim would attempt to get the picture when "Fred" would come to me. It worked!

Amazing as it may seem, the bird returned to that same area every winter for three years. Then came a cold, barren winter with little snow. He didn't appear. I realized that without snow he had easy access to food in the woods. I continued to try without success, but I got a complete surprise that fall.

We were camping late that year in October. Afternoons were cool enough for us to enjoy a campfire by the trailer. The sound and warmth of a crackling fire along with the sight and smells of a sunny fall day were super. I noticed a blue jay high up in the surrounding trees. He was soon joined by two companions.

With nothing to lose and noticing how big the main bird seemed, I resorted to my Fred-feeding strategy. He came to me. He used the grab-and-fly technique. I could tell the other two birds wanted desperately to join the parade but couldn't quite bring themselves to actual human contact. I could put food close to me, but they could not bring themselves to take it from my hand. In the meantime, Fred was soon establishing new precedents. He graduated from snatch and run to settling eventually on my outstretched hand and eating right there. What a feeling! Excitement, trust, and intrigue all at the same time.

He had his ground rules as well. He would stay as long as I maintained eye contact. If I looked away, even for a second, he would leave. Our routine was steady. One of us would see the other. He would fly from tree to tree, knowing the flutter would make me aware of his presence. I would put food in my outstretched hand and call him. I was even able to get him to come once for a visitor to witness what few would believe. I got the same response the next fall, without a winter encounter.

This year, we had our fall rendezvous for one day only. I had seven years of a totally unique experience—one that provided fond memories for both Jim and me…and some inside information on how to make friends with a blue jay.

Did You Know?

Blue jays do great impersonations of hawks.

Blue jay migratory patterns are erratic and unpredictable. Even a bird that winters south one year might stay north the next.

Despite a bad reputation for eating the eggs of other birds, blue jays eat mostly insects and nuts.

Encounter with the Great Eastern Black Bear

The Cape Breton Highlands National Park area is world renowned for its scenic ocean beauty, beautiful autumn colors, and splendid wilderness. Although my husband Jim and I had spent much time there in the early nineties—our hearts were truly "in the Highlands"—we hadn't had the opportunity to go there for several years.

Like most people in the East, we had never considered the black bear to be a dangerous animal. We would hear of serious attacks in Western Canada and the United States but somehow didn't associate with them. Due to the amount of time we spent in the woods, we had already had some bear encounters and indeed had a great deal of respect, always giving them a wide berth and following appropriate encounter protocols.

For instance, during my first encounter while traveling along a dirt road, both the driver and I spotted a large female crossing right in front of us. We stopped to look and, just as we were speeding up to continue our journey, I spotted two small cubs in the middle of the road. Wary that the driver might not have seen them, I yelled loudly to stop—with quick results. The feeling of excitement was palpable. I grabbed my camera and opened the car door. Before my foot hit the road, the driver grabbed me and planted me back in my passenger seat. "Never come between a mother bear and her cubs," my companion said. I listened. We stayed inside the car and watched the cubs scamper across to join their mother. They looked so cuddly, but they were danger in disguise. Perhaps it was my imagination but, as we drove away, the female stopped, turned around, and gave us one last look—as if to thank us for letting her babies come safely across. It gave me a good feeling to help take the edge off the stern lecture.

Back to the Highlands. Jim and I left Halifax early in the morning and, for the first time, decided to take our trailer. Suffice to say it was not an easy drive, and we were both overjoyed when we arrived to get the trailer set up. It had been a most unusual year with a fall explosion of spring black flies. I was not impressed with that situation. They were so prolific one could inhale them if you stayed outside for any length of time. So much for the barbeque; to keep moving was the order of the day. The first evening was spent enjoying the beauty of the area and the lovely sunset—all from the car, of course, in order to avoid those unseasonable black flies.

The following morning, we got packed and ready early. Our plan was to take one of our favorite mountain hikes and begin a search for a male moose. Although I had several moose pictures in my portfolio, I had heard there were amazing moose in that area, much larger than those I had recorded. Water and apples in hand, we began our ascent at 8:30 a.m. That was the last shred of sanity for the morning.

We hiked silently up the trail, which is great if you want to see a moose but deadly if you are in a bear's domain. The hike was listed as one of the more strenuous trails. I could feel my boots slipping over the wet rocks as we continued our ascent. There was a continuous sound of the trickle of water, which is classic of damp, rocky terrain. One can actually smell the dark dampness along these narrow difficult paths. Moose scat was noticeable all along the trail but, as we reached the summit, I hadn't any luck spotting a moose.

Plan B was to take some scenic pictures of the Cabot Trail from the mountain peak, which consisted of a rather narrow area with a rest bench. It had a wonderful view of the trail but was accessible only by coming around a blind turn at the very top.

The photographer always hikes in front. Under normal circumstances, an animal usually flees within seconds of sighting of the first person. I was walking approximately six to eight feet in front of my faithful hiking partner. Coming around the blind corner of the summit, I came eye to eye with a large male black bear that was situated to the left of the bench.

The moment froze. A million thoughts went flying through my mind simultaneously—the first one being what a precarious situation this was. Oddly enough, my initial reaction was a loss of hearing. It was as if I was suspended in time and space. My instincts were torn in two: one to get out of there as quickly as possible, the other to think, "This is the chance of a lifetime to get a picture of a wild black bear." As the situation unfolded, I realized I would never again want to be in that situation.

Jim tells me he saw the bear within milliseconds of my own sighting and had begun talking very quietly to me. I did not knowingly hear him; time stood still for me at that moment. Whether his words were sinking in subliminally or whether I simply decided to "go for it," we will never know. Apparently he had given me a "go ahead" to take the picture, but I was in that eerie zone, totally transfixed with what I was facing.

Bottom line: I reached down slowly and extracted my camera from my waist pack. The bear was roughly only 20 feet away from me at this point and in a grove of fir trees. I took focus but, as I did, he turned his face away from me as if to tell me I had better not still be there when he turned back. I stood my ground, knowing my only chance to get him would be waiting until he turned back. He did turn his face back, and the look I saw as I focused on his face—one I will never forget—seemed to be one of total disgust, displeasure oozing from those cold black eyes. As I took the picture, I could almost feel hatred in those eyes, right through the lens of my camera.

The click of the camera should have spooked him, and Jim and I both fully expected him to flee. He stood his ground.

At that point, I was so fully in the moment, focusing to try to get another picture, until I became aware of Jim's voice telling me to back up. He repeated himself one more time before I realized our precarious position, so I began backing up until he got me positioned behind him. Since Jim is much taller than I, the bear could not see me then. It had also started coming towards us. We knew we had to get out of this horrible situation.

The path was very serpentine, so we paused at the first corner. Once again, our rapport was tested as I attempted to get our only knife out of the backpack Jim was wearing. There were too many pockets to search. We had to put our unspoken emergency plan into action. Our sensitivities were being pressed. As much as I didn't want to, I had to leave him and hike as fast as I could to get help. He had to remain, walking backwards slowly.

The bear was stalking us steadily, so Jim had to keep the animal in his sights without making direct eye contact—while maintaining a steady pace to get out of the bear's territory. Once a person comes in contact with a bear in the wild, whatever ensues is in the bear's control totally, and this bear was not reacting normally. (Looking back on it now, I jokingly say, "He didn't read the bear rule book." But it was no joke at the time.)

I remember trying desperately to hike quickly without running. I could hear Jim well behind me saying, "You have to go faster." The gravity of our situation really hit me then, an actual physical reaction starting in the pit of my stomach—fear, and the beginnings of panic—that I could actually taste. I became painfully aware that if the bear could sense this from me, the situation would only worsen. I had to get angry with myself to keep my cool.

Unknown to me, Jim was watching the bear stalking us and trying urgently to put more distance between the animal and us.

What I had surmised when I had taken the picture was that the bear had been standing up, when in fact he had been lying down. He had stood up once I had started the retreat.

The sight Jim was dealing with was of those great huge paws, one crossing over the other as the bear followed us. This frightening situation continued for almost half a kilometer, my heart sinking and my stomach turning. We crossed the summit of that mountain in record time. A hike that normally would have been difficult and awkward seemed to disappear beneath our feet.

On the descent and well within the danger zone, we came upon a young female tourist hiking alone. She did not speak fluent English but responded well to my terse description of the impending danger. Ironically, my tone of voice and my body language seemed to get the message across quickly. She handled it well, turned around quickly, and joined us in our retreat. (She later told us she detected the scent of the bear as she was ascending, but didn't know what animal she was dealing with.)

The next predicament was a young couple also making the ascent. We explained the situation to them both as quickly as possible, knowing that time was of the essence and this was now the second delay. The woman responded quickly, but the man was reluctant initially to turn around. Thankfully, he joined us.

It was a strange and rapid descent. For the first few kilometers, not a word was spoken. The sound of our footsteps echoed against the damp rock walls of the narrow, rocky cliff trail.

We will never be sure what finally discouraged the animal to give up the hunt. Perhaps we left his territory, or it might have been the sound of so many humans in one group. He could have simply given up on the chase. The park warden of the area suggested the main factor that might have prevented him from charging at us was the serpentine direction of the trail; he couldn't get a straight run at us.

The trail, for the first time in our memory, was closed down for two days. The wardens searched for the bear and found signs, but they were unable to sight or capture him.

We learned a lot from this adventure and are thankful no harm came to us or to the young people we brought down the mountain that fateful day. I will no longer actively seek out black bears. It is a misconception there are no dangerous bears in the Maritimes.

The warden seemed to coin the situation most accurately. His indications to us were that one in one hundred black bears are unpredictable and will chase humans rather than run from them. The problem this; when you do encounter a bear in the woods, you simply don't know which number you've drawn.

Did You Know?

The American black bear is found exclusively in North America.

A group of bears is called a sloth, after the Middle English word *slowthe* (slow)—something black bears are not.

The heaviest bear on record weighed 880 pounds, well above the 125- to 500-pound average.

The Crow Caper

West Nile Virus furor: high priority in the summer season, particularly in wooded areas. National parks are no exception, and we were enjoying ourselves at one of our favorites. Thankfully for us, this particular area had no reports of that problem, but the shadow of the threat was constantly on everyone's mind—especially in the woods.

Park interpreters are some of the key people keeping their hands on the pulse of park activities. Over many years of frequenting the parks, we had developed a pleasant, enjoyable, and informative relationship with many of them.

Early morning is the best time to embark on a day of hiking. The scent and freshness of the dew hangs still in the air. The possibility of an animal sighting is much higher. Awareness of sounds and scents seem to be much more acute. I readily detect the rustle of a bird in the deep woods. A squirrel running along the ground seemingly makes the noise of a huge moose. I notice the wetness of the wild grass. The same moisture seems to give added luster to the multicolored wildflowers. There even seems to be an enhancement to the wild berries, like the blueberries just coming into season.

Away we went on one of our favorite back roads within the park. This particular road was closed off shortly past the entrance. We would park the car across the main highway, hike the main road for about one kilometer then down the unpaved back road to a closure site where the "real" hiking begins. Along the road, there would often be signs of wild animals, but never an actual encounter. Bird sightings would be fleeting. Crows, of course, are amongst the quickest to take flight, always trumpeting their loud "caw" as they leave.

On this particular day, we came upon a crow on the dirt road just before the wood barrier of the closure. Immediately we saw strange behavior. As we approached, it didn't fly away. Instead, it walked haphazardly on the road while its mate watched from a nearby tree. The mate kept calling to it, as if concerned for its welfare and faithfully standing by, which also surprised me. Upon closer inspection, the crow's feathers looked slightly wet, as if sweaty. I got the sneaking suspicion this was not a normal scene. We noticed what seemed to be regurgitated food on the road. I immediately became concerned. Cautious deliberation led me to decide, if the crow was still there when we returned, we would definitely reassess the situation. We continued along our way, and I forgot about it. After all, it wasn't an outstanding situation, however strange. Crows also can be very bold when it comes to food. The concept of one overeating to the point of becoming sick was not beyond the realm of possibility.

This park is for hiking, so there's little level ground. Downhill would appear to be easy but does require its own technique to avoid painful shin splints. Then, of course, there's the loop at the bottom and the return trip up the adjoining hill, which is shorter but steeper.

Within a few steps, the steepness of the slopes engages our bodies, and immediately we begin to sweat to keep up the pace. The tug of gravity is constant; keeping up the pace becomes a challenge. We have to choose our water stops wisely and ensure we don't stay long to avoid cooling off.

Upon return to the same site, the crow was still there, along with obvious signs of vomiting and diarrhea. That was it for me. I was determined to alert the park interpreters at the nearest kiosk. Jim tried to slow me down, suggesting we discuss what we saw before pressing the West Nile "panic button."

Before the words were out of his mouth, like a bad kid I left him and turned directly into the kiosk. Without hesitation, I reported a crow exhibiting signs of West Nile infection. Keeping in mind the great rapport I had with the staff, my credibility was solid. The young staffer in question immediately got on the two-way radio and called the report in, asking at the same time for a ranger to go to the scene to investigate our findings. I felt fully vindicated; my bemused partner was left smiling, shaking his head.

Once over with, the whole situation was dropped from my mind. We were back at our trailer getting cleaned up and ready to go into the nearest town when I heard voices just outside the trailer door. This was unusual. My initial thought: "Was I driving too fast through the park compound?"

No sense hiding in the trailer, I came out to face the music. There was the head warden engrossed in conversation with Jim. This was a man who had been a senior ranger; his picture was a common sight Canada wide in numerous publications. Apprehension overcame me, feelings ranging from concern and fear to being aghast.

He turned to me and said in the most formal of tones, "Pardon me, ma'am, was it you that reported the crow?"

I was shocked. I replied, "Yes," and he proceeded to tell me—with a slightly amused smile—that rarely, but on occasion, crows will eat unripe blueberries. Immature crows especially fall prey to that mistake. He had seen it himself very few times in all his years of experience. The result of that intake in their stomach literally renders them " intoxicated," which is exactly what the ranger took wry pleasure in telling me had occurred in this instance.

This was too much. One has to appreciate a scene in which a (literally) famous senior park warden tells you to your face that you've been duped by a drunken crow. How embarrassing is that? Suffice to say, it was all Jim could do to maintain a straight face. My initial response was to hope the earth would swallow me up!

Here is where the great camaraderie with the park staff came back to bite me. As I stood there, a car rolled past, friendly park staff with heads out of windows emitting drunken caws as they drove by. The senior ranger was pleased to play the straight man.

For the rest of our stay that summer, I was never allowed to live it down. There's something to be said for a good sense of humor and an ability to laugh at oneself. In the meantime, the next time I see a drunken crow, I will walk directly past any kiosk, say hello to my friends, and stick to telling my unbelievable drunken crow story!

Did You Know?

Sioux tradition tells of a white crow that scared away the buffalo before hunters could kill them. In retaliation, a warrior threw the crow into the fire—and crows have been black ever since.

Ravens are the crows' closest genetic relatives, but Jays, Jackdaws, Magpies and others are also cousins. Crows are found everywhere in the world, except New Zealand, South America, and Antarctica.

The Phenomenon

Picture this: sitting alone by a small rustic cove along the uninhabited shoreline of a protected lake.

Once you have made the short but rugged trek through the thick woods to get there, you sit and your body begins to unwind. A sense of relaxation slowly sets in. With this mellow state comes a sharpening of perception. Sitting at the waters edge is similar to sitting at a nature play. On a sunny day, you will get a double dose of sun due to the reflection from the water. It is not uncommon to burn even through a bug net jacket!

The wind begins its daily morning acceleration and gusts through the leaves in the trees, making a friendly sound that sparkles in your ears and makes dimples on the bright blue water. In that moment, the solitude becomes less lonely and more comforting.

One of my most common summer activities is seeking out the loon—a water bird that has always held a particular allure for me, with its haunting cry and unusual and beautiful plumage. Its early return to the wilderness is always such a welcome sign of spring. With that in mind, I have always given full credit to my husband Jim's patience when, time after time, I leave for the lakes where they dwell. Then come the ensuing hours I spend just waiting for them to go swimming by elegantly.

At times I get so caught up in the beauty around me that my mind drifts—until suddenly a loon pops out of the water directly in front of me, startling me to the point of adrenaline rush! Sometimes it would be like a comedic skit with me jumping in one direction and the loon flapping in escape to the other.

I sit in various places for hours at a time, camera in hand, hoping for that great shot. Naturally, with every shot I get, the bar goes higher to get an even better shot. There is an old expression that begins, "If I had a dime for every time…"

It was a typical summer last year. I had already begun my annual vigil for the loons at a lake where I knew they nested. Their prime nesting time is during black fly and mosquito season. Needless to say, spending wait time at a lakeside only increases exposure to these pests. This particular day was no exception. The order of the day was black flies—clouds of them. I was dressed in fly netting head to toe. In the warm late-spring temperature, I was anything but comfortable. I was located in a fairly wild area with a small clearing and an old picnic bench. To sit at the bench simply made me an easy target for heat and black flies. After waiting a while without a successful sighting, I decided to sit on the ground, firmly situated in my "niche" on shore.

Loons are particularly adverse to predators, including humans, when they are nesting. I knew I had a long wait on my hands to see just one of them. Since the weeds and wild grass were wet, I decided to sit on the bare ground in hopes of escaping the heat and flies. My location also lowered my profile so the loons would not sense my presence, hence giving me a photo opportunity. I was thankful the mosquitoes weren't out at the time, as the sun was rising and the comfort level was already dropping.

I looked around on the ground to see if there was anything interesting to take a picture of. As I became more sensitive to my surroundings, I noticed a dragonfly on a nearby blade of grass. Staring at this fascinating creature, I realized it must have just emerged from its cocoon. The wings were still stuck together, glistening in the sunlight. Its body wobbled back and forth when the wind caught the grass. As it hung on, waiting for the sun and breeze to dry it out, I sensed a delicate, fragile balance in the struggle for survival. I moved back quickly, not wanting to disturb it. The next sitting spot presented yet another dragonfly coming out of that birth-like stupor. My eyes almost seemed to tune in to my surroundings at a totally different level, as if I had awoken and begun to see that small area in its true totality for the very first time. My vision had developed a new level of sensitivity.

Suddenly, all the grass in that small area seemed to be moving. Initially, the hair on the back of my neck began to rise. Then I saw what was really happening. There were hundreds of blades of grass with innumerable dragonflies coming out of their cocoons—a massive, communal birth of a whole generation of these fascinating creatures.

Not expecting anything near this magnitude, I did not have the proper camera equipment to capture this happening. Off I scrambled through the woods back to the car, grabbed more equipment then ran back through the woods. It was very difficult trying to capture the actual feel of that event on film; these delicate creatures blended so well with their environment (which was no accident).

I took many pictures that day. With great regret, I realized I was alone. This would have been a standalone experience to share with others, such a spectacular and eerie sight—one that may never be seen in a lifetime!

Then came the defining moment as I suddenly sensed the presence of another entity. Just as the dragonflies had emerged from their vegetative state, I heard a familiar hum. Thousands of mosquitoes appeared as if on cue and out of nowhere, ready to serve as a food source for the newborn dragonflies. The whole experience gave me a rejuvenated respect for Mother Nature. This was nature at its most amazing—a true phenomenon!

Did You Know?

Dragonflies aren't flies. Dragonflies have four wings, while flies only have two.

Dragonflies have been around for over 300 million years—since before dinosaurs roamed the earth.

The damselfly is a smaller, more delicate version of the dragonfly. Both belong to the order *Odonata*.

Getting Up Close and Personal with a Moose

He stands just 10 feet from me, weighing at least 1,500 pounds. As I look him square in the eye, my initial feelings are of total awe and disbelief. Is it possible to be that close to a 24-point bull moose?

My husband Jim and I had spent many vacations and done a lot of hiking in the Cape Breton Highlands. There is a well-known song written about this area called "My Heart's in the Highlands." A little part of our hearts will always be there. We had taken a five-year hiatus from our trips to the area and finally had decided to haul our trailer to stay in the park campground for a change. I was so excited about going down to get the fall colors, classic highland scenery, and wildlife on film.

Having been successful with some pictures of moose in other areas in the Maritimes, my goal was to find some larger animals. Most in the portfolio were immature and had not been receptive or approachable.

My enthusiasm for the species included going to a seminar on moose delivered by a wildlife biologist. He stated clearly that most moose in the Atlantic area weighed about 800 pounds maximum.

On previous visits many years ago, Jim had seen uncommonly large moose. He felt if we could locate the strategic area, I would see moose much larger than those shown at the seminar. Those that I had already sighted in other parks seemed enormous, and they were well below the 800-pound range.

The second evening—after mellowing out and getting acclimatized—we decided to take a drive outside the local community. I spotted a beautiful sunset with shades of pastel pink and blue. It was a classic fall evening, and many tourists lined the road.

Enthusiastically, I jumped out of our truck and was lining up a picture when I heard Jim calling to me. In my total absorption with the colors of the sunset against the foam of the breaking surf, I had walked past a huge bull moose in the thickets by the road. A group of tourists jostled, many trying to get a picture of him in the approaching dusk. The feeling amongst the group was of total excitement, but it soon became obvious this was beginning to agitate the great beast. He moved quickly from thicket to thicket, constantly changing elevations.

The first problem I encountered was the height of this magnificent creature. At best, my lens captured his legs and nothing more.

A palpable sense of camaraderie had developed amongst the group. We tried a number of innovative approaches in a desperate attempt to get a picture before it got too dark—including putting a young boy on Jim's shoulders to take a snap—all to no avail.

Looking back on that evening, one of the memories that stick in my mind is that of an American man standing next to me as we watched the moose. He murmured, "The only shooting that should take place around a creature this magnificent is that of a camera." I had to agree.

The following morning, we went back to the same area and found clear signs of the moose but no sighting. I could sense his presence. The large area where he had slept clearly showed the imprint of his body, and of course there was the telltale scat outside his secluded area.

We came back that same evening. This time a female came out. She was impressive but was much more timid and left the area quickly. I was becoming discouraged. The big bull was obviously there because the female was frequenting the area. However, there seemed to be no set time or pattern.

The next day, as I came out of my early morning stupor—still in the "fuzzy zone"—my partner burst in. He had risen early, gone back to the same location, and spotted the big male. I got dressed as quickly as possible, grabbed my camera, and we sped back to the strategic location.

There was no sign of the moose anywhere. We decided to walk in through the area in hopes of getting lucky.

The terrain intimidated me. The thickets were over my head, restricting my line of sight. Not being able to see overhead leaves me with a feeling of helplessness and frustration, giving me some understanding as to how people get lost in the woods.

As we turned to go back to the truck, Jim spotted a big moose rack moving along the top of the thickets at the crest of a knoll on our left. There he was! I got my camera out and took one shot. This moose was not impressed; he soon put distance between us.

Suddenly, there was another bull! They were both grazing in the same thicket—unheard of! I got one picture of them back to back, their rumps only feet apart. They were both so large they could barely fit in one frame. It was obvious the one that wasn't impressed with us was quite a bit older than the other. Both moose had huge racks. If only I could get a good close up of them.

It was the same situation as the previous evening—my being too short and they're being so big. To complicate things further, the high thickets prevented me from seeing them at all once they shuffled away. The older moose left as soon as he spotted me. Jim valiantly tried beating the bushes to spy the younger moose, and I became painfully aware of the danger of our situation. We decided to head back to the truck and attempt to get a picture from the safety of the open tailgate.

The moose did come out but was still too tall to ensure a good picture, dictating a climb to the roof of the truck. I didn't know which was scarier, being on the roof of a one-ton truck or being on the ground with a full-grown bull moose.

Once I shot some pictures with great difficulty, a local man appeared on the scene. He was obviously amused at the sight of a grown woman, camera in hand, standing on the roof of a truck. "You're pretty brave", he remarked. "You can come down, the moose aren't rutting yet".

I was only too glad to come down, jumping to the ground in a flash. In the meantime, Jim had continued his efforts to get the bull to come into a clearer area. In the process, he struck up a conversation with our newfound friend and gave one more effort to entice the moose into a nearby clearing. He told me to go there and wait. I experienced an air of excitement and anticipation.

Branched snapped audibly, followed by a crashing sound.

Feelings can change rapidly at a time like this and they did—to anxiety. If the animal was running, would I be in its path?

No more than ten feet dead ahead of me, looking right at me, was our moose. I overcame my awe and shot a whole role of film within minutes. His rack was so big it could barely fit into the picture frame. He tolerated me as I shot picture after picture. He seemed content to concentrate on grazing the young growth on the thickets. Each time his head came up, I took another angle. The top of my head did not even reach his butt. What an incredible feeling. Then, as quickly as he appeared, he slipped silently away.

It had all transpired in less than an hour. To me the time had seemed endless, although a sense of sadness set in when he was gone. Through all these proceedings, Jim and "friend" were standing close by, monitoring all events. They too were overwhelmed with the moose's acceptance of my presence and the length of time the photo shoot encompassed.

I learned later that day that the moose was approximately 1,500 pounds and still in velvet—to me, that has got to be the most beautiful phase. Apparently there are moose in that area weighing more. This certainly insures another trip back to the Highlands for us!

❧ ❧

Did You Know?

Moose have 27 pairs of chromosomes—four more than humans.

"Moose" comes from the Algonquin word *mooswa* ("twig eater" or "animal that strips bark off trees").

Only the bull (male) moose grows antlers. (Reindeer, on the other hand, don't discriminate.)

The Uncommon Loon

One of the most distinctive wilderness sounds is the compelling call of the loon. Hearing that unique call brings mixed feelings of fascination, eeriness, and a distinct sense of solitude. The particular species that frequents my favorite areas is called the Common Loon. However, there is nothing "common" about this beautiful water bird. I was fortunate enough to encounter a display of courage and tenacity that would bespeak a much larger and more formidable species.

Every year, I look forward to locating loons on the lakes my husband and I frequent while backcountry camping, canoeing, hiking, or just simply enjoying the great outdoors. Wilderness camping is one of my favorite activities. Miles away from any form of communication, you find a sense of tranquility and quietness that can be found in no other place. The plain physical exertion leaves you in a state of tiredness that promotes awareness of the sights, smells, and sounds of the forest and the elements.

It was one of those years when moving the trailer began early. We headed to one of our favorite parks and were set up in May. It didn't take me very long to locate a lake hosting loons. The location was within reasonable driving distance from our trailer, so I decided very early to attempt to get a picture of loon chicks—a tough, if not impossible, job.

One thing to be said for my setting the bar so high that year; an intensive learning experience about this remarkable creature was about to begin. We first discovered these loons while on an evening drive as at least five loons called and seemingly played, swimming and diving. We never knew there they would pop up, since they could cover vast distances of the lake with one dive. There were times, as I sat quietly by the shore, that one would pop up and we would both jump, one as startled as the other.

Once I had a lake, my next move was to find a secluded spot to observe without disturbing them and hopefully get a location where they were nesting. Time after time, I went back to my little spot. They seemed to take great delight in staying just out of range then diving to the other end of the lake, leaving me with the distinct feeling they were simply having great fun outsmarting me.

I observed them for about three weeks, talked to some seasoned staff at a local park, and learned where they were nesting. Once a loon couple nests, other loons tend to stay away from that lake. My lighthearted encounters began to diminish drastically.

I was also not alone in my efforts. One day, while waiting in the woods at lakeside, camera in hand, I heard a loud noise from the woods just behind me. It was a researcher whose project for that year was to observe the loon couple on the very lake I had chosen. We exchanged greetings and both went our separate ways.

June came and went without any sign of activity around the nest site. This left me with an acute sense of disappointment and a feeling of apprehension; perhaps something had gone amiss. I was giving up.

One day, the woods rustled behind me. The researcher was back. This time she informed me that, indeed, the loons had nested. A predator had destroyed the eggs; the remains of the shells had washed up on the shore. My worst fears confirmed, my immediate instinct was anger. Who could have committed such a heartless act? Was it man or predator? No wonder those beautiful birds avoided me. It seemed they had good reason to be distrustful.

The good news was that they had built another nest in a totally different area. Loons always return to the same nest site every year, so this was a massive effort for them, not counting the lateness of the season and the difficulty they would have in laying another set of eggs and getting the chicks ready in time for the winter migration. All involved in the observation were now very concerned.

For me, my hopes of getting a picture of the family were pretty well dashed. The nest was in completely inaccessible terrain. I couldn't get a glimpse of the area even with my most powerful lens. Would they even be successful in laying another two eggs?

Then came my so-called "brilliant" idea.

To see the loons without compromising their required privacy, I purchased a small children's inflatable swimming device. Since the device was boat shaped and I was an avid canoeist, I figured this would be easy.

The inflation process alone should have tipped me off. Blowing up the device was tough, leaving me short of breath, cranky, and far too warm. Then there was the fact the device was awkward and anything but waterproof. I later realized I was lucky not to have ruined my camera equipment.

Having dropped me off to begin the adventure, my partner in plan shook his head in laughter and disbelief as he walked away. We had a prearranged reconnaissance time. I put the device in the water, stashed my gear, and got in. When I was no more than three feet from the shore, the breeze came up. The boat took flight at the mercy of the wind, hurtling its way rapidly along the lake. No paddle in the world was going to turn this toy around!

The wind blew me all the way down to the other end of the lake, which was comprised of total swamp and wilderness. There was no getting out onto the shore in this terrain. Worse, there was absolutely no sign of loons of any kind, as if they had never frequented this lake.

The long arduous process of paddling back up the lake against the wind began. Why did I get myself into this ridiculous situation? Frustration and chagrin set in during my embattled trip back to the launch site—which took an hour. I was beat, the air was too hot and the sun blinding. I dragged myself up onto the shore, got my gear out, and waited for my husband.

I looked across the lake, just shaking my head at my folly when, as if out of nowhere, I saw a lone male loon swimming up the middle of the lake. He called. Directly across the lake one large and two small dots appeared on the horizon. They came towards me, getting bigger and bigger—the female with two little chicks in tow, swimming freely on their own. They came up to within 15 feet of me. I reached for my camera, fearing my movement might scare them away.

The female was feeding the chicks, diving and returning with small perch that she gently placed in each chick's mouth. She seemed oblivious to my presence. I was transfixed. Simultaneously, my husband appeared, along with the researcher and a colleague. We all watched, motionless, as this mother loon fed her chicks (I later learned they were only five days old).

The researcher leaned over and whispered to me that I would probably never get that close to a wild loon again in my lifetime. (At the time, I had no appreciation for the accuracy of that remark.) The moment was so filled with excitement, everyone totally silent and motionless. My hands were shaking as I tried to hold the lens steady. The mother loon moved the chicks slowly away with the male loon breaking new ground for them and standing guard at the same time. Another rarity: both parents together coaching the young chicks. Time was of the essence.

The next morning, I went back to the same place in hope of seeing them under less chaotic circumstances. As I broke through the underbrush, I could see them all together, floating as if suspended in the water just for that split second. I took one picture before the male spotted me. They moved away, slowly but deliberately. I was never to get a glimpse of them together or that close again.

It is my understanding that the chicks did survive to migrate that year. The parent loons never again returned to the original nest. They continued to nest in that unseen far away place.

I hear them call, see them changing guard, and continue to hope, perhaps, to get another chance to see young chicks. But at least I know they managed to raise that one tiny family against all odds.

Did You Know?

The loon is famous for mating for life, but recent studies show a loon may take more than one mate during its life.

In 1987, the Royal Canadian Mint introduced the new one-dollar coin, the back of which featured a finely rendered image of the Common Loon. The image, combined with initial public resistance to the idea of replacing the paper dollar, led to the coin being called a "loonie."

The unmistakable call of the loon is often compared to a yodel or a laugh.

There's a Raccoon in the Woodpile

Living in an unfinished house many years ago with young children around, we had lots of backyard trees and a large set of sliding doors in the dining room. These doors, which would normally lead onto an outdoor deck, instead led to a 10-foot drop to the wooded ground below. I affectionately called it "the mother-in-law" door! In those days, it was not unheard of for children to throw scraps of food out that door to see "who" would show up. Of course, the first "who" was a raccoon. The woods were so thick that there was a permanent family in residence, producing a litter of baby raccoons every year.

It didn't take very long for them to put the house on their list of regular nocturnal visits. (That was before the days of animal-carried diseases.) I found them entrancing, getting to the point of being able to hand feed them. Their little paws, even though reinforced with claws, felt like velvet as they took the food from my hand so timidly and gently.

Many years have passed, and in these days of dwindling natural forests, raccoons have developed a bad reputation, perhaps because they seem to adapt easily to an environment that is inhabited by people. This is not their first choice; it tends to happen when humans move into their habitat. In a camping situation, it is definitely the latter.

It was early fall when we made our migration back to Nova Scotia, hoping to enjoy nature's most beautiful time of the year with its brilliant colors along with the smell of fallen leaves and crisp cool mornings. I noticed when we set our trailer up that the lids of nearby garbage cans were tied to the handles. This was new to us, and a forewarning of what was to come.

Nighttime. Just before falling asleep, I heard an enormous crash followed by half an hour of crashing and banging. When we awoke the next morning, all the garbage can lids were removed and the cans were lying on their sides. The odor of garbage permeated the air. Initially puzzled, we soon realized it was our old friend, the raccoon.

Exploring the situation, we found out that there were many raccoons, traveling in groups, going from area to area looking for food. Apparently, they frequent different areas each year. This year just happened to be our area, and the problem was much more pronounced than usual. Was this indicative of a hard winter? I had never seen this much activity before. We were in for quite a treat. To save our sleep, I decided to put a large rock on top of our designated can.

Sitting around a nice campfire is one of the attributes of camping most campers enjoy thoroughly. In the chill of the morning, it is comforting to sit in front of that fire, feeling the warmth of the crackling flames and drinking that first cup of coffee or perhaps hot chocolate. In the night, the fire appeals to that inner sense that seems built in—being attracted to the light and warmth of the campfire, perhaps to roast marshmallows or wieners.

A week after our arrival, well past dusk, the flames of the fire lit up our area in the warm, still autumn dark. We kept a small woodpile by the firebox, with a tarpaulin close by behind our seats for those rainy nights. As we sat by our campfire, I became aware of a presence behind the tarp. I nudged my husband Jim and we went into our standard "animal alert" mode. We waited for what seemed a long time then, slowly but surely, a little fat fluffy gray body with big shiny yellow eyes came carefully around the woodpile—a long and timid trip for him, moving only an inch at a time. I was impressed with the superb condition of his shiny coat and how very cute he looked.

As I spoke softly to him, he seemed to sense we would not harm him. He didn't run. Obviously a very young animal, this might have been his first night away from the den and his parents. Other raccoons we had seen to that time had fled quickly at first sight. This was completely different.

We continued to talk to him, threw him a few tidbits, and he nestled down in the leaves about 10 feet directly in front of us. Entranced with this situation, I could have stayed for a long time; however, it was getting late and time for bed. When we stood up, he left. I figured that would be the last of him. I was wrong.

The next night, apprehensive but hopeful, the campfire ablaze, we settled into our camp chairs. Much to our delight, we heard that little rustle behind the tarp and out he came, a little braver this time but still incredibly timid. We talked to him gently, and he got a little more comfortable. He graced us with a 20-minute visit that night, ambling away just before bedtime. I decided to call him "Jud" and hoped this would not be our last meeting.

Sure as autumn leaves in October, he was back on night three. To have three nights in a row without rain is good luck anywhere when camping. His third visit was a total kick to me. I'd read that these creatures would tame easily but under much different circumstances. This was a wild raccoon, and I knew his family was still around; we could hear them through the night at other sites. They are very loud and quarrelsome amongst each other, emitting loud catlike snarls and howls. It can be outright scary! We were amazed at his faithfulness.

On night three, he arrived at his usual time but somehow the atmosphere was different. He had much less fear of us. We were able to get up out of our camp chairs and he didn't leave. In fact, he didn't move. The most remarkable thing was that he would follow me around when I did get up. Most impressively, when I needed something from the truck, he would get up on the running board when I opened the door. I know he would have gotten in!

We said our goodnights and went into the trailer, but my curiosity was piqued. Looking out the window, I could see him curled up under the bottom step of the trailer. Surely he had adopted us. My heart melted. I knew he would have to be discouraged. That thought alone saddened me. I would begin the withdrawal the next fireside night—an uninviting task.

Night four was yet another clear night. With heavy heart, I kept vigil by our fire. No sign of Jud. How strange.

We were never to see him again, at least not the way he behaved with us those precious evenings. Raccoons did run through our campsite off and on through the night for the duration of that fall, usually very late. If one of us opened the trailer door, they would flee.

What happened to our little friend? Did he go back to the den and get a reprimand from his parents? Perhaps he had been estranged from his group and reunited with them, adopting their normal wild habits. We will never know and can only hope, wherever he went, he was happy and healthy. The one thing known for sure was he gave us three wonderful nights of contact in the most pristine style. To this day, when I hear a little noise in the late evening by the campfire, I watch expectantly for those bright yellow eyes and still hope to see a cute, grey, furry, chubby animal with a little mask—if only to say hello and watch him disappear back into the forest with his friends.

Did You Know?

The most common diseases in raccoons are rabies and distemper.
Mature raccoons become very ill tempered if they cannot mate.
Raccoon comes from the Algonquin word *arakun*, meaning "one who scratches with his hands."

Have You Ever Seen a Snapping Turtle?

Its tail is jagged and saw-toothed, and it has a rugged exterior shell that, in older specimens, can become pockmarked and thick. If approached, it may open its large gaping mouth, hissing loudly and aggressively. Even the smallest of the adults will shake violently if you attempt to pick it up. This is the description of a modern day dinosaur: the snapping turtle.

I had seen and taken pictures of many creatures in the wild. A two-person team, my husband Jim and I have a standard wilderness camping routine. A normal year would usually allow us one of those camping trips—always a treasured event. I'd photographed painted turtles in the more frequented areas, and this was the only species I had seen in the wild.

During childhood, there was the standard procedure of pestering my parents for a pet turtle in the plastic bowl with the little ramp and palm tree in the middle. These turtles were no bigger than the diameter of an average cucumber. I remember how smelly the dish would get, with my parents holding out for me to do the cleaning. It was "my" pet; hence, my responsibility. In the summers when we went family camping, I invariably took the turtle with me and it somehow always escaped and headed for the lake. Before the end of summer, every one of them would have gotten away, never to be seen again. The operative question: "Did they survive?" I thought not at the time, since these were tropical turtles, and heading for the wild in the Atlantic Provinces really didn't seem like a safe bet.

That was the extent of my exposure to turtles until our highly anticipated trip to the wilderness for the current year. On this particular backcountry trip, we went into the wilderness farther than in previous years. This was really exciting. In usual style, arrival at our destination was by canoe—no easy feat when traveling long distances. We arrived at the campsite, and I couldn't wait to go back out onto the lake. As soon as the tent was set up and supplies put away, I went back to the launch site on the lake's edge. Evening was just setting in on a nice sunny day without too much wind. The camp was positioned in a well-protected cove. I stepped out onto a large rock to get a better view.

The lake was flat, shiny, and glistening blue in the evening sun. There appeared a slight bump on the surface of the water. Was it a plant? Perhaps it was the tip of a submerged piece of waterlogged wood; I made a mental note so we wouldn't get stuck on it in the canoe. Time passed as I stood there, just taking all the beauty in. Oddly enough the little bump seemed to be closer. My curiosity stirred, observation set in.

Suddenly, the bump disappeared. Strange. Then it reappeared. Turning back to our campsite to get an audience, I relayed what had occurred. Jim came down to the water's edge. Sure enough, the bump was still there. "That's a turtle," he said. I was fascinated. What type of turtle could this be? Jim went back to start the campfire, leaving me by the water's edge, my curiosity tweaked.

It didn't take very long for some action. The bump became an obvious nose, one that continued to come closer and closer. Within a few minutes, a turtle was visible—and big! The so-called nose had been just the tip of the nose of a snapping turtle, probably about 40 pounds and the first one I had ever seen. It came closer and closer. As I called to my husband, I couldn't help feeling nervous. Would this big creature bite me?

There was a wry little smile on Jim's face when he told me there was no danger of being bitten. He had seen numerous snappers and was familiar with their behavior.

Armed with what were supposedly my turtle facts, I hopped back onto my lookout rock. This turtle had no fear as it continued to come forward. Within a few short seconds, he climbed up on the rock and opened his mouth to take a nice bite of my sneaker-clad foot. Horror set in. Then as quickly as he had opened his mouth he closed it, but not on my foot. He didn't bite, he simply retreated back into the water.

In the meantime, the fountain of information—otherwise known as Jim—had come down again. I turned and immediately saw a big grin. "They hate the smell of rubber," he said, indicating the soles of my sneakers.

I put a big note on my get-even list.

This was the beginning of a fascinating opportunity to get a look at turtle behavior. Before we left that site, our big snapper came back with a friend and also others of different smaller species, mostly painted turtles. In the evening after supper, we would go to the shore and sit quietly. Before long, the little noses would pop up. A person not familiar with the sight would never know those tiny projections were turtles. It provided quite a show.

The experience gave us fodder for a lot of fun storytelling over the years. I had been leery of swimming in the same water those turtles frequented at that time, and there were questions left unanswered. They remained unanswered until several years later during another wilderness camping trip.

The site chosen then was well traveled. On our second day there, we had visitors: a young couple who were camping across the same lake. We enjoyed their company, swapping stories around the campfire and savoring the warm calm evening.

In the midst of an engrossing conversation, the young man pointed out a terrible scar on the calf of one of his legs and told us of a camping experience he had in Ontario several years ago. He, too, had an encounter with a snapping turtle. His experience, however, was not the lighthearted experience ours had been. He disregarded the size of the animal and the fact he was in water that was the turtle's habitat. He did decide to go swimming. To his horror the big snapper in question bit him. The result: a large piece out of his calf and the ensuing scar.

We were shocked, but the story did accomplish one thing. Having wondered about that aspect of dealing with these animals, we increased our understanding. Unfortunate it had to be at our friend's expense.

These days, we give snapping turtles due respect with distance. They are the closest things to prehistoric beasts I have ever seen, from thick, scaled shell to saw-toothed tail—which looks so similar to pictures I have seen of dinosaurs. Their jaws are incredibly powerful. Since our experience with them, I have seen a whole duck disappear suddenly while floating along the surface of a lake, captured by a big snapping turtle. When approached on land a female will often stand her ground and hiss—a scary sight and sound.

I have a great deal of respect for these animals. Now, when I see a little nose poking out of the water at a local swimming hole, I am always sure to check if it's one of our "prehistoric" friends.

Did You Know?

The average weight of a snapping turtle is 35 to 45 pounds.

Snappers have keen senses: taste, sight and sense are all very good.

Snapper shells are actually brown; they only appear green due to algae growth.

The Alien Moth

What comes to mind when a person thinks of beauty? A material object such as jewelry? Perhaps a child, a painting, a view of nature in some form, or a butterfly? The world is filled with beauty. Is it conceivable the word would be associated with a moth?

I have a favorite saying involving the hour my husband arises in the morning. "He gets the birds up then the birds proceed to wake the people up." It's been a family joke for years, but there are times when these early risings pay off.

On one particular morning, well into the summer season during a stay in New Brunswick, Jim was up before dawn with his usual flair. The normal routine would be to slip away for a drive to enjoy the sunrise and whatever creatures he would see during his travels. Many times, his explorations would lead me to a great tip for a picture.

That morning, he came back in a hurry and woke me quickly from my early morning stupor. I could vaguely hear the words, "You have to get up and see this!" Startling for the first words of the day. Apparently, in his rambling he had stumbled upon a huge moth and had managed to coax it, with a little gentle help, close to our campsite.

My immediate thought was, "Is this necessary? A moth? What could be so special about an insect?" I was inclined to roll over and go back to sleep. Some extra urgency in his voice prevented me from doing that.

I got up and wobbled down the steps to the great outdoors. There in the nearby bushes in the early morning light was the largest winged insect I had ever seen in my life. Even though its wings were tight together, it was obvious this was an extremely colorful species. I scrambled back into the trailer to grab my camera, hoping desperately this unusual creature would still be there. The light was poor and the grass still wet with dew.

I observed it closely during camera setup; it was obviously in quite a weakened condition. Initially, it clung to the leaves of the bush with its wings folded tightly. How was I going to get a picture that would do justice to the majesty of this huge moth?

While all the technical thoughts were rolling through my mind, the moth opened its wings slowly. Time to move in for the picture. Moving around the moth as carefully as possible and focusing the lens, I noticed this species was so large that it actually had feathers on its antennae!

Getting into my usual routine of trying different angles, I approached the moth closer and closer. As I did, its wings opened fully, revealing the most beautifully intricate colorful pattern. The wingspan appeared to be eight inches from tip to tip. I opened my hand for comparison. To my amazement, the moth was the same size as my spread fingers—the biggest moth I had ever seen! The coloration of its outstretched wings reminded me of an intricate Indian Navaho blanket. The detail in its markings was fascinating. I took several pictures and hoped the moth would survive. It was unlike anything encountered before or since.

I thought perhaps it had hitchhiked on a tour bus or trailer that had come from a faraway place. Certainly that would explain the standalone appearance and the weakness it displayed.

My picture taking completed, we retired to the trailer. Upon returning shortly after, we found no trace of our lovely visitor. Hopefully, it had fluttered away to live out its lifecycle in the local forest.

Then the real mystery began.

First, would the photos turn out? I was definitely not in prime picture taking form at that moment. The light conditions were also very poor. Would there be positive results? Thankfully, when the pictures were developed, they came out with all detail intact. We were delighted and curious at the same time. The persistent question remained. What was it?

The season ended, and we came home for the winter. I began what was to become an arduous task of trying to find out what this moth was. I had submitted the information to some of the appropriate people of that area without any luck. Then I resorted to the standard Internet search. That rendered me more frustrated than informed. It seemed as if the search for the moth's identity was turning into mission: impossible. Convinced the creature wasn't local or common to the area, and factoring in where we discovered it and the lack of identification, we decided, laughingly, to name it "The Alien Moth."

Tracking and identifying this creature had become a veritable puzzle. I talked to various people about this moth, but my efforts inevitably led to dead ends. My notorious early riser approached several seasoned travelers, picture in hand, without luck. During the winter, my encounters with nature enthusiasts also left me empty handed. I even mounted an 8x10 portrait of the moth to lend out to an art gallery.

Eight months later, we had almost given up. One stormbound afternoon in March, the standard computer search was on: "outsized moths." Hope was not high on the horizon; we had spent hours searching the Internet for any moth that resembled our unusual find. Thank goodness we had evidence in the picture.

As I turned to the wood stove to warm my hands, I heard an almost inaudible "I think I've found it." The early riser had come to the rescue again!

There it was in all its glory: a silk moth, sometimes commonly called the Robin moth.. How ironic. The silkworm is renowned for being an ugly, greedy, unattractive creature, but it produces one of our most beautiful commodities: silk. Even as a moth, this insect is not ordinarily considered in the same appealing league as the butterfly. Yet this moth was the most beautiful winged insect I had ever seen.

In pursuing some knowledge of this moth, I learned we were fortunate to have seen it. In the Eastern Canadian range, sightings are normally fleeting, usually of the moth in flight. To have seen it so close and still in all its glory was almost a gift—as if it had just fluttered out of some remote tropical rainforest.

Did You Know?

The wingspan of the silkmoth can grow up to almost six inches.
Adult silkmoths do not feed; they have no mouths.
Silkmoths are *not* considered an endangered species.

The Mexican Standoff

Whitetail deer have always been a beautiful animal to me. Their numbers wax and wane in each deer-bearing province of Canada, dependent on many factors, including the harshness of the winter, the number of predators, and the luck of local hunters.

Like people, these animals each have their own personalities along with classic behaviors indicative of the species. This is what makes them intriguing. These gentle animals will approach so quietly at times if you are sitting still in the deep woods; one could be standing directly behind you and you would not be aware.

I had that experience multifold while waiting at dusk for a glimpse of a lone buck. Sitting quietly under a large tree, I became alert to something behind me. Turning around slowly, I saw five doe within 10 feet. They stared solemnly, as if trying to decide what to make of me. I remained motionless. Their relentless sense of curiosity moved them forward, albeit cautiously. Perhaps they were deciding to include me in their group. It was an outstanding feeling, sitting in their midst for at least 20 minutes. Their eyes were so compelling, large, and soft. Gradually, one by one, they moved away.

My photo collection of these intriguing creatures seems to get larger every year. There is one very difficult picture to obtain—that of the buck with his fall and winter horns, commonly known as a rack. Despite a catalogue of wonderful pictures of does, fawn, yearlings, spikes, and males in the spring, popular demand for pictures by far favors the buck with a rack.

One of my favorite jokes is that of being able to sell a picture of just the rack, no visible deer attached!

To this end, I began what was to become years of hunting for a buck—armed only with a camera. Picture a petite woman clad in forest friendly colors mentally reviewing all the hunters' "tips and tricks"—all to find that elusive, rare buck. Many were the times when I'd been snuggled into ditches along the road, hidden behind trees in meadows, and sometimes just walking the edges of secondary roads. I would manage to give some innocent passerby a near heart attack at the sight of a woman in full camouflage. My forays have given me grist for many funny stories, but also made me the butt of many jokes. On one occasion, I actually made it to the airwaves of a two-way radio after startling some workers monitoring a local area.

Deer can also give a person quite a start. During one of my camouflage capers, I became airborne one early, chilly autumn morning. Waiting silently for a buck sighting, I was unaware of a big doe that had slipped up directly behind me. With a stamp of her hoof and a very loud snort, she not only scared me half to death but let me know, in no uncertain terms, she wanted me out of there!

In one of our favorite fall hiking/biking areas, my husband and I had heard from some national park staff that a buck was frequenting a popular camping area near a lake and a playground. Deciding to start my early morning stakeouts here, I chose to position myself at the top of the hill in a lush meadow. A dirt road and a path through the woods led down to the parking lot below.

Morning after morning, I dragged myself out of bed at the chilly crack of dawn, only to look down at a motionless tree line at the bottom of that meadow. The steam from the lake behind me rose in the early morning frost. The lake had that thin skin of ice that rendered it perfectly calm and would melt with the rapidly rising sun. Dawn colors assume an eerie glow in that frosty air, yielding a beauty only seen in the first rays of sun at that time of year. I had to force myself away from the tranquility of simply allowing myself to stay there, taking in the sunrise.

I came close to giving up but, on the fourth morning, a young buck came out of the trees. He spotted me immediately; there was no chance to get my camera out or focused. The time spent waiting began to pay off in terms of familiarity of the area. The terrain was unique and inclusive. Having spent many hours waiting, I'd canvassed it extensively, taking in the mellow fall smells and following trails through the woods to the road and the parking lot.

First thought through my mind: "Where is he going to go?" Intuition told me he would try to head through the woods to the parking lot in his attempt to get away from the area. As a general rule, no matter what the season, does tend to be less timid than bucks. During the fall mating season, males become almost invisible.

I headed quickly and quietly down the dirt road leading to that very parking lot. Trees lined the road, twisting and converging with the hiking path that led to the playground equipment on the sandy beach. At the convergence, I looked towards the lake then up at the hiking path. Simultaneously, the young buck had walked down and was looking at me.

When he spotted me, he had one foreleg up in classic flight position. Ironically, I was also in mid step. There we were, eye to eye, each with a foot off the ground. Needless to say, the four-legged buck definitely had an advantage. Standing on one leg with a heavy camera in my hands was not a good development. It wasn't long before I started to wobble, my leg and arms tiring as I attempted to keep my balance without making a sound. The realization set in quickly as I ran out of ability to stand on one leg. This was a classic "Mexican Standoff."

With great good luck on my side, the buck decided to break the standoff. He proceeded to come down the path towards me. I knew if I held my ground, he would have to pass in front of me. This was the critical moment! I took a deep breath, moved my raised leg slowly to the ground, and remained motionless.

We looked at each other. He came forward and began to walk across my path. Wonderful! He passed directly in front of me with that beautiful lake in the background. He walked past the swings and slides of the playground. Once more we stared at each other, almost as if he were deciding "friend or foe." He got to the road then turned around as if to give me one last look. Was he was aware how much I appreciated his beauty?

Savoring the moment, I watched him walk slowly away. Not wanting to frighten him, I remained at my post, hoping to garner a chance for another encounter in future years.

Did You Know?

This animal is the most widely distributed of all North America's large animals, with one of the largest populations.

A deer's tail has a broad base and is almost a foot long.

Male deer frequently exceed three feet at shoulder height and 220 pounds in weight.